THE BOOK OF CALM

LIZZIE CORNWALL

THE BOOK OF CALM

With research by Anna Caffyn and Lexie Harris

Summersdale Publishers Ltd
46 West Street
Chichester
West Sussex
PO19 1RP
UK

www.summersdale.com

Printed and bound in China

ISBN: 978-1-84953-597-7

To..

From..

We have more possibilities available in each moment than we realise.

Thích Nhất Hạnh

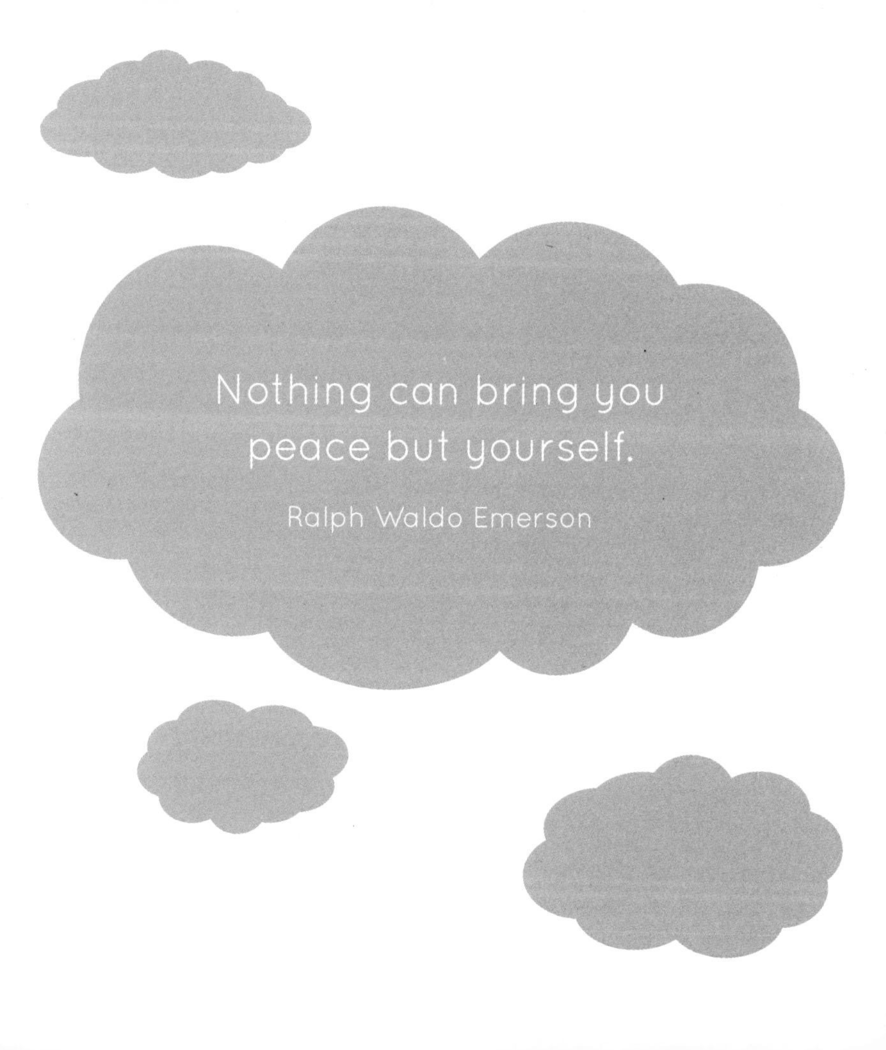
Nothing can bring you
peace but yourself.
Ralph Waldo Emerson

CLOSE YOUR EYES AND
FOCUS ON YOUR BREATHING.
DON'T TRY TO CHANGE IT,
SIMPLY BE AWARE OF IT.

Each one has to find his
peace from within. And peace to
be real must be unaffected by
outside circumstances.

Mahatma Gandhi

The future starts today, not tomorrow.

Pope John Paul II

IF YOU LET GO OF
WORRY, YOUR DREAMS
CAN FLY FREE.

Give me odorous at sunrise a garden of beautiful flowers where I can walk undisturbed.

Walt Whitman

There is a wisdom of the head, and... a wisdom of the heart.

Charles Dickens

You're only here for a short visit. Don't hurry, don't worry. And be sure to smell the flowers along the way.

Walter Hagen

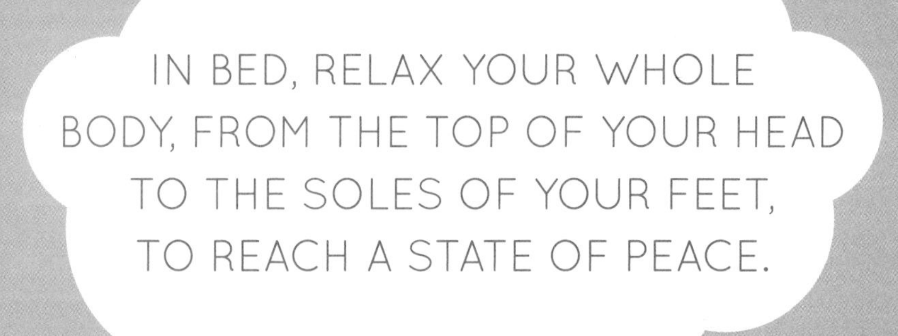
IN BED, RELAX YOUR WHOLE
BODY, FROM THE TOP OF YOUR HEAD
TO THE SOLES OF YOUR FEET,
TO REACH A STATE OF PEACE.

SIMPLE ACTS OF
KINDNESS BRING
HAPPINESS AND CALM.

He who has a Why? in life can
tolerate almost any How?

Friedrich Nietzsche

TILT YOUR HEAD AND WATCH
THE CLOUDS DRIFTING BY.
IMAGINE YOURSELF FLOATING
ALONG WITH THEM.

The most important thing is
to enjoy your life – to be happy –
it's all that matters.

Audrey Hepburn

Meditation is the tongue of the soul
and the language of our spirit.

Jeremy Taylor

THERE IS NO ONE WHO CAN TELL YOU WHO TO BE… EXCEPT YOURSELF.

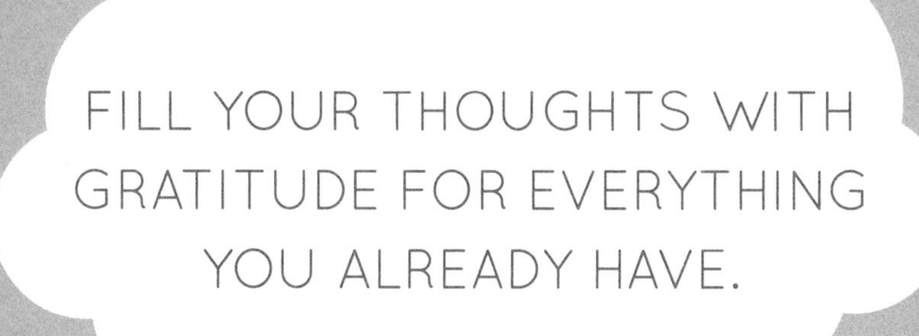
FILL YOUR THOUGHTS WITH
GRATITUDE FOR EVERYTHING
YOU ALREADY HAVE.

Confine yourself
to the present.

Marcus Aurelius

Self-confidence is the first requisite to great undertakings.

Samuel Johnson

A CLEAR MIND IS THE KEY TO A SIMPLE LIFE.

All, everything that I understand,
I understand only because I love.

Leo Tolstoy

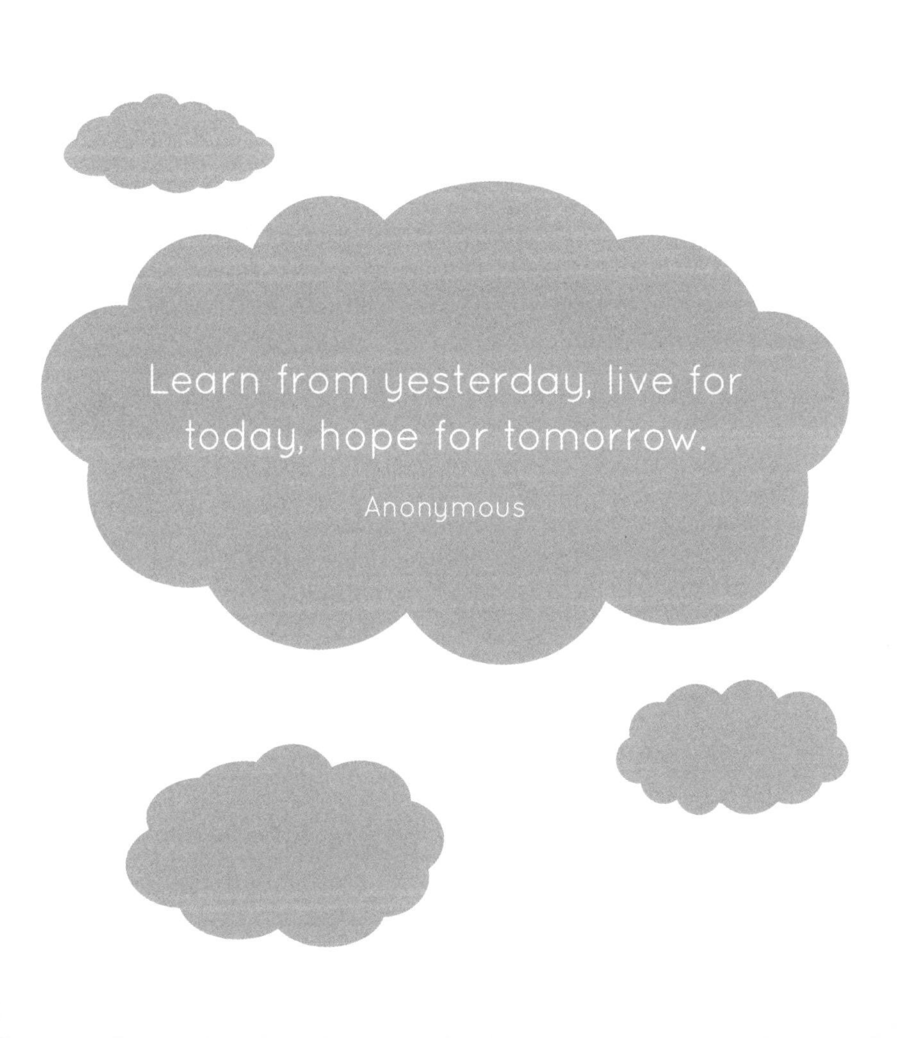
Learn from yesterday, live for
today, hope for tomorrow.
Anonymous

Happiness is the
harvest of a quiet eye.

Austin O'Malley

SPRING CLEAN YOUR HOME. TIDYING YOUR SURROUNDINGS WILL HELP TO CLEAR YOUR MIND.

BREATHE, RELAX.

Every breath we take, every step we make, can be filled with peace, joy and serenity.

Thích Nhất Hạnh

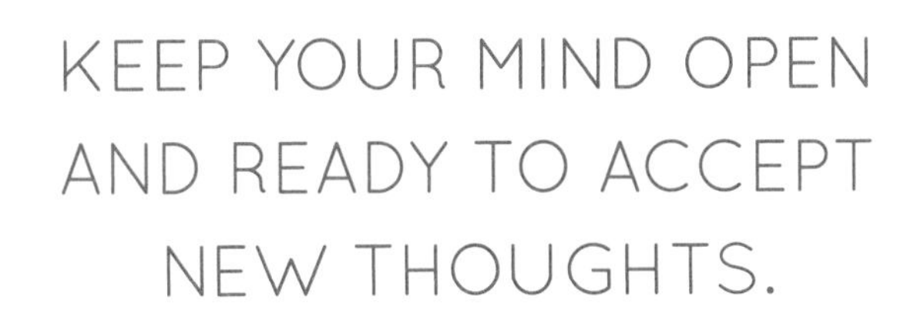
KEEP YOUR MIND OPEN
AND READY TO ACCEPT
NEW THOUGHTS.

Happiness in this world,
when it comes, comes incidentally.
Make it the object of pursuit, and it
leads us a wild-goose chase,
and is never attained.

Nathaniel Hawthorne

All things share the same
breath – the beast, the tree,
the man… the air shares its spirit
with all the life it supports.

Chief Seattle

FREE YOURSELF FROM
SELF-JUDGEMENT –
ACCEPT YOURSELF
AS YOU ARE.

BE PRESENT IN THIS MOMENT AND IMMERSE YOURSELF WITHIN IT.

When I was living in
solitude... I noticed how the
monotony of a quiet life
stimulates the creative mind.

Albert Einstein

Let your soul stand cool
and composed before a
million universes.

Walt Whitman

WHATEVER HAS HAPPENED IN THE PAST, YOU CAN ALWAYS TAKE A FRESH STEP INTO A FUTURE FULL OF NEW HOPES.

Very little is needed to make
a happy life; it is all within yourself,
in your way of thinking.

Marcus Aurelius

Spread love everywhere you go... Let no one ever come to you without leaving happier.

Mother Teresa

Remember when
life's path is steep to
keep your mind even.

Horace

IN THE SHOWER, ALLOW YOURSELF TO FOCUS ON THE SENSATION OF WARM WATER ON YOUR SKIN.

SURROUND YOURSELF
WITH POSITIVE PEOPLE
WHO BRING CALMNESS
INTO YOUR LIFE.

Calm can solve
all issues.

Pope Shenouda III

ON A SUNNY DAY, CLOSE YOUR EYES AND TAKE PLEASURE IN THE WARMTH OF THE SUN'S RAYS ON YOUR FACE.

How calm,
how beautiful comes on
The stilly hour when
storms are gone!

Thomas Moore

The quality, not the longevity,
of one's life is what is important.

Martin Luther King Jr

BELIEVE IN YOURSELF.

TAKE YOUR THOUGHTS ON A VISIT TO A HAPPY MEMORY, WITH ALL ITS SIGHTS AND SOUNDS.

To thine own self be true,
And it must follow,
as the night the day,
Thou canst not then be
false to any man.

William Shakespeare

An early-morning walk is a blessing for the whole day.

Henry David Thoreau

LET GO OF WHAT
YOU CAN'T CONTROL.

The time to relax is when
you don't have time for it.

Sydney J. Harris

I meditate so I know how to find a peaceful place within to be calm and peaceful.

Roseanne Barr

Believe that life is worth living and your belief will help create the fact.

William James

WRAP YOUR HANDS AROUND
A WARM CUP OF TEA, CLOSE
YOUR EYES AND ENJOY BREATHING
IN THE STEAM BEFORE YOU
TAKE YOUR FIRST SIP.

LISTEN TO YOUR HEART.

Dreams are today's answers to tomorrow's questions.

Edgar Cayce

LET YOURSELF BE MESMERISED BY THE MOVEMENT OF WATER IN A STREAM, RIVER, POND OR LAKE.

Learn to calm down the
winds of your mind, and you
will enjoy great inner peace.

Remez Sasson

Yesterday is but today's memory, and tomorrow is today's dream.

Khalil Gibran

BE AT PEACE
WITH YOURSELF.

OPEN YOUR WINDOWS
AND FEEL THE COOL,
GENTLE BREEZE CARESS
YOUR SKIN.

We must let go of the life
we have planned, so as to accept
the one that is waiting for us.

Joseph Campbell

Genius is
eternal patience.

Michelangelo

KEEP AN OPEN MIND.

The highest perfection of
human life consists in the mind of
man being detached from care.

Thomas Aquinas

The ideal of calm exists
in a sitting cat.
Jules Renard

To me, every hour of the
light and dark is a miracle.

Walt Whitman

PLACE THREE FINGERS OF
EACH HAND ON YOUR TEMPLES
AND GENTLY MASSAGE AWAY
ANY TENSION.

LET YOURSELF
MOVE FORWARD.

After a storm comes a calm.

Matthew Henry

LIE DOWN AND LISTEN TO
SOOTHING MUSIC OR JUST
ENJOY THE SILENCE.

Wherever you are –
be all there.

Anonymous

The purpose of our lives
is to be happy.

Dalai Lama

YOU'RE NEVER LOST, YOU'RE JUST DISCOVERING NEW PLACES.

TAKE A PEN AND LET IT GLIDE ACROSS THE PAPER. DRAW WHATEVER COMES FROM WITHIN.

After all, the best thing one can do when it's raining is to let it rain.

Henry Wadsworth Longfellow

We must use time wisely and
forever realise that the time is
always ripe to do right.

Nelson Mandela

ANGER IS A WEIGHT THAT HOLDS US DOWN. ALLOW YOURSELF TO CUT THE STRINGS AND FLOAT FREE OF IT.

Calmness of mind
is one of the beautiful
jewels of wisdom.

James Allen

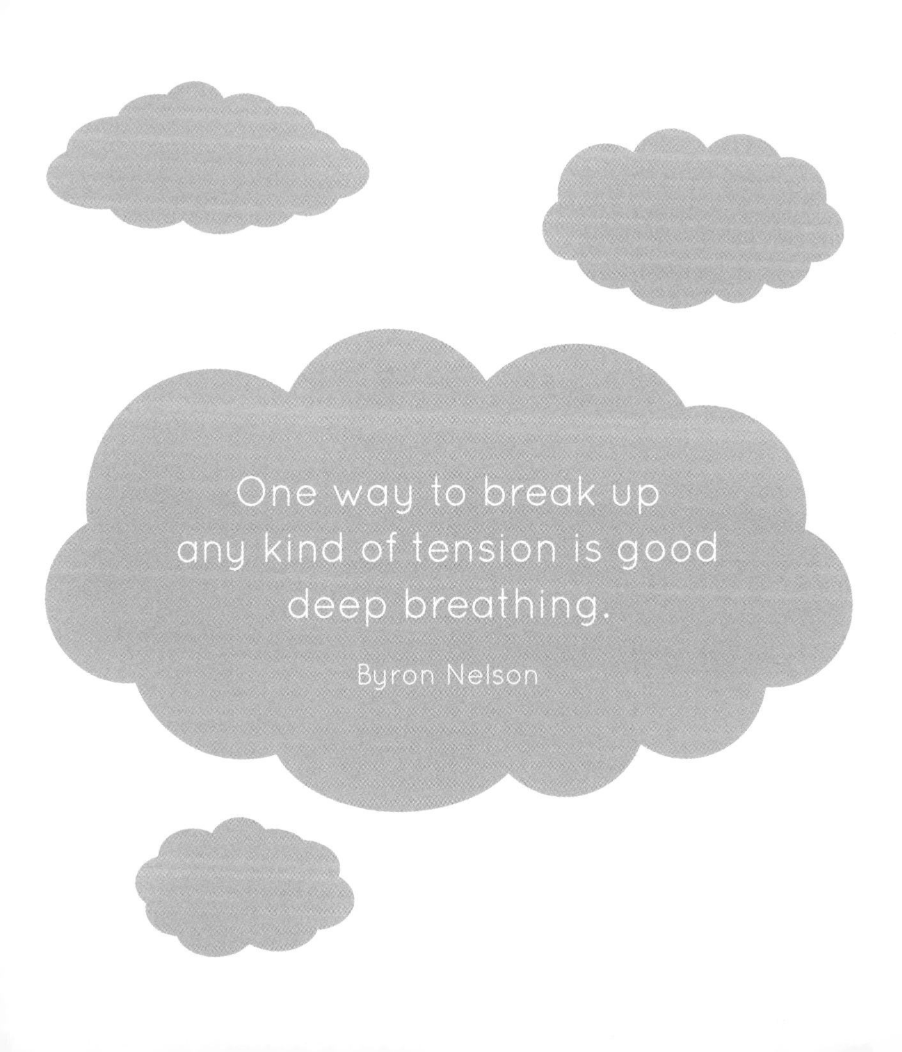
One way to break up
any kind of tension is good
deep breathing.
Byron Nelson

I hope for nothing. I fear nothing. I am free.

Nikos Kazantzakis

VISUALISE A PEACEFUL
SCENE AND ALLOW YOURSELF
TO ENJOY BEING THERE.

IF YOU LOVE WHAT YOU DO, YOU CAN ACHIEVE ANYTHING.

When I let go of what I am,
I become what I might be.

Lao Tzu

ON A CLOUDLESS DAY,
LIE BACK AND LOSE YOURSELF
IN THE PERFECT BLUE.

There is a calmness to a life lived in gratitude, a quiet joy.

Ralph H. Blum

Your mind will answer most questions if you learn to relax and wait for the answer.

William S. Burroughs

WHEN FACED WITH
CHANGE, LOOK FOR
THE POSITIVE SIDE AND
SEE THE POTENTIAL.

VISIT PLACES WHERE
YOU FIND YOURSELF AT PEACE,
SUCH AS A BEACH, A MEADOW,
A SWIMMING POOL OR EVEN
YOUR BACK GARDEN.

Be happy with what you have and are, be generous with both, and you won't have to hunt for happiness.

William Ewart Gladstone

When you are content to
be simply yourself and don't
compare or compete, everybody
will respect you.

Lao Tzu

DON'T RACE FOR THE FINISH LINE – ENJOY THE JOURNEY.

With the past, I have nothing to do; nor with the future. I live now.

Ralph Waldo Emerson

If you do what you love,
it is the best way to relax.
Christian Louboutin

The greatest self is a
peaceful smile, that always
sees the world smiling back.

Bryant H. McGill

GIVE YOURSELF TIME EACH DAY TO ENJOY A QUIET PURSUIT, SUCH AS READING A BOOK OR PRACTISING A CRAFT.

IF YOU DON'T LIKE IT,
YOU DON'T HAVE
TO PURSUE IT.

Clouds come floating into
my life, no longer to carry rain
or usher storm, but to add
colour to my sunset sky.

Rabindranath Tagore

TAKE A MOMENT JUST
TO BREATHE AND EXIST, FEEL
YOURSELF TAKING UP SPACE IN THE
ENORMOUSNESS OF THE UNIVERSE
AND CONSIDER THE IMPORTANCE
YOU HAVE AS A BEING.

Never be in a hurry;
do everything quietly
and in a calm spirit.

Francis de Sales

Our freedom can be measured by the number of things we can walk away from.

Vernon Howard

BE TRUE TO YOURSELF.

SPENDING TIME IN NATURE, ALLOWING YOURSELF TO BE ENFOLDED IN ITS PRESENCE, WILL BRING YOU CALM.

Let go of the past, let go of the future, let go of the present, and cross over to the farther shore of existence.

Buddha

Be happy for this moment. This moment is your life.

Omar Khayyám

IF YOU FOCUS
ON LIFE'S POSITIVES,
THE NEGATIVES WILL
FADE AWAY.

Everything comes to us that belongs to us if we create the capacity to receive it.

Rabindranath Tagore

Peace is its own reward.

Nelson Mandela

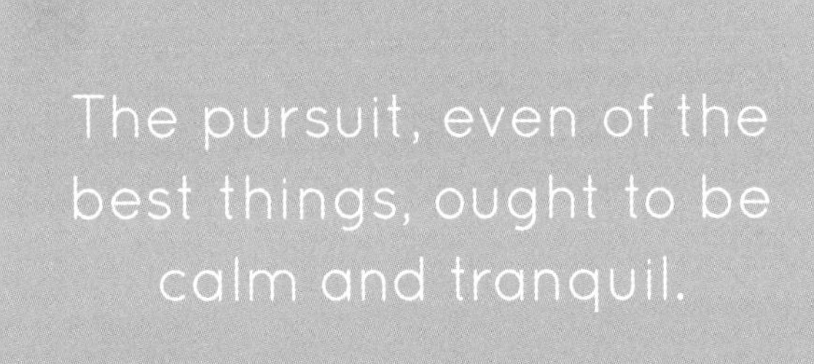

The pursuit, even of the best things, ought to be calm and tranquil.

Marcus Tullius Cicero

SMILE – A POSITIVE ATTITUDE
IS CONTAGIOUS.

DON'T LOOK BACK,
YOU'RE NOT GOING
THAT WAY.

Compassion, tolerance,
forgiveness and a sense of
self-discipline are qualities that
help us lead our daily lives
with a calm mind.

Dalai Lama

FOCUS ON WHAT IS
AHEAD OF YOU, NOT
WHAT HAS PASSED.

A cloudy day is no match for a sunny disposition.

William Arthur Ward

No great work has ever been produced except after a long interval of still and musing meditation.

Walter Bagehot

TRY LIVING AT A SLOWER PACE.

LAUGH – NOTHING
FEELS BETTER.

Remain calm, serene,
always in command of yourself.
You will then find out how easy
it is to get along.

Paramahansa Yogananda

The privilege of a lifetime is being who you are.

Joseph Campbell

KEEP YOUR HEAD
UP AND YOUR
HEART OPEN.

Silence is the element in which great things fashion themselves together.

Thomas Carlyle

Our entire life consists
ultimately in accepting
ourselves as we are.
Jean Anouilh

If the mind is calm,
your spontaneity and honest
thoughts appear. You become
more spontaneous.

Chade-Meng Tan

TURN OFF ANY DEVICES AND DISCONNECT YOURSELF FROM THE OUTSIDE WORLD, EVEN IF IT'S ONLY FOR TEN MINUTES.

THE BEST IS
YET TO COME.

A quiet mind cureth all.

Robert Burton